You Can't Take YOUR BODY TO A CAR MECHANIC!

A Book About WHAT MAKES YOU SICK

Fred Ehrlich

pictures by Amanda Haley

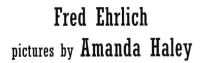

BLUE APPLE

For John Moses, M.D.
—F.M.E.

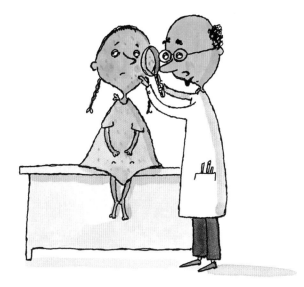

Text copyright © 2004, 2014 by Fred Ehrlich
Illustrations copyright © 2004, 2014 by Amanda Haley
All rights reserved
CIP data is available

Published in the United States 2014 by
Blue Apple Books
515 Valley Street, Maplewood, N J 07040
www.blueapplebooks.com

First Edition
Printed in China
ISBN: 978-1-60905-452-6

1 3 5 7 9 10 8 6 4 2

Contents

What Makes You Sick

When there's trouble with a car, it sometimes makes a funny noise. Sometimes it won't run at all. Your mom or dad calls the mechanic.

When there's trouble inside your body, you develop symptoms—perhaps a headache or vomiting. The symptoms are your body's way of letting you know that it's fighting an illness.

But you can't take your body to a car mechanic when you are sick. Sometimes your mom or dad will take you to a doctor; most of the time, you get better on your own. When the trouble is fixed, the symptoms go away and you feel well again.

Germs

Germs make you sick. There are two kinds of germs—bacteria and viruses. There are hundreds of each kind, and every year scientists make new discoveries linking certain diseases to specific bacteria or viruses.

The first bacteria was discovered in 1683, and with the discovery of penicillin in 1928, doctors learned how to treat many bacterial diseases.

Viruses were discovered after bacteria in 1880, and they are harder to isolate and find treatment for.

CHAPTER ONE
Vomiting, Diarrhea & Other Digestive Troubles

Bellyache

A bellyache is usually a crampy pain. Sometimes vomiting and/or diarrhea comes with it. Spoiled food, a virus, a bacteria—all of these can give you a bellyache.

Sister says I'm looking green.
She wants to calm my fears.
"Don't worry if your lunch returns.
It won't come out your ears."

When things are working right, the food you swallow goes through a tube, called the esophagus, into your stomach. There it is mixed with strong chemicals and churned around until it is soft and mostly liquid.

Then it is squeezed, bit by bit, into the small intestine.

Usually you don't notice your stomach when it is doing its work. But sometimes it sends an unpleasant message: "Something is very wrong down here!" The food reverses direction and comes flying out of your mouth. In other words, you vomit.

Why should your stomach throw your food back out? Well, you may have eaten food that is spoiled, which is full of bacteria. Or, if you have a fever, the vomiting is probably caused by a virus or other germs.

If your lunch is forgotten,
It will surely grow rotten.
Leave it in the cafeteria,
And it will grow bacteria.

Carsickness can also cause vomiting. The motion of a car can disturb your sense of balance, causing nausea. Carsickness sometimes happens during long, boring, twisty car rides. Its purpose is to spread vomit all over the back seat of the car, so that parents learn a lesson about long, boring car rides!

Diarrhea

Bowel movements, or poop, remind us that although we are human beings who wear clothes and have lots of fine thoughts, we are also animals. We need to eat, digest, and use some of the digested food for energy, then get rid of the leftovers.

Sometimes things go wrong. Instead of taking its time in the usual way, the bowel speeds up and squirts out watery poop—preferably into the toilet.

The same things that cause vomiting cause diarrhea: bacteria in spoiled food and viruses. Now for some good news: long, boring, twisty car rides do NOT cause diarrhea!

My belly is painfully gurgling.
I hope that a toilet is near.
I fear that everything in me
Is about to shoot out of my rear!

CHAPTER TWO

The Common Cold & Other Common Problems

Colds

Colds are caused by a virus. The symptoms are sneezing, stuffy nose, and sometimes a cough. Children usually have four to six colds a year.

Many different viruses cause colds. Because a cold is not caused by just one kind of germ, you can catch colds over and over again.

One of the unpleasant symptoms that comes with a cold is mucus. Sometimes mucus is thin and watery; sometimes it's thick and yellow. The yellow stuff has bacteria.

Some mucus is green.
Some mucus is yellow.
When my nose is full of mucus,
I'm a most disgusting fellow!

My dose is aw stupped up,
And I cannot taste my food.
Everyone stay away—
Or else you'll be ACHOOD!

Laryngitis

When you have a cold, your vocal cords may swell up, which changes the usual sound of your voice.
You have laryngitis.

Sometimes you cannot make any sound at all and you may say, "I've lost my voice."

I have no voice!

What?

Ted has laryngitis.
He sounds strange, of course.
Maybe Ted should try to neigh,
Since he is a little hoarse!

Earache

When you have a cold, the small tubes that go from your throat to your ears get swollen. Fluid collects in the middle ear. Bacteria grow in the fluid, and this causes swelling and pain—and earache!

Earache, earache, go away.

Don't come back another day!

Sore Throat

Some sore throats are caused by viruses; others are caused by bacteria. Your doctor may sometimes touch the back of your throat with a cotton swab to get some of the germs to study. The lab test is called a "throat culture."

William has a red throat.
His tonsils are big and sore.
When the doctor says, "Say AHHH!"
He'd like to yell, "No more!"

Flu

When someone has a cold and fever, it is usually called "the flu." The real name for flu is influenza, which is a serious illness that most people don't have when they say, "I have the flu." There are different flu viruses. Sometimes people get flu shots to prevent them from getting sick.

We're all in bed with pains in the head.
The whole family is down with the flu.
We've got fevers and aches, shivers and shakes.
I hope you don't catch it, too!

Headache

Everyone gets a headache at some time or other. Most sicknesses that cause fever also give you a headache.

Often we can't explain why someone has a headache. Other pains in the body—especially a bellyache—are like that, too. Sometimes they just seem to happen.

Parents often think that headaches and bellyaches are reported to them by kids who would like to stay home from school. Sound familiar?

Headaches make Daddy grumpy.
Headaches make me mad.
If I don't want to go to school,
Mommy says, "Too bad!"

CHAPTER THREE

Zits, Warts & Other Skin Troubles Caused by Germs

A car with "skin troubles" (dings, dents, and scrapes) goes to the body shop. A child with skin trouble goes to a pediatrician, or maybe to a dermatologist, a doctor who specializes in diseases of the skin.

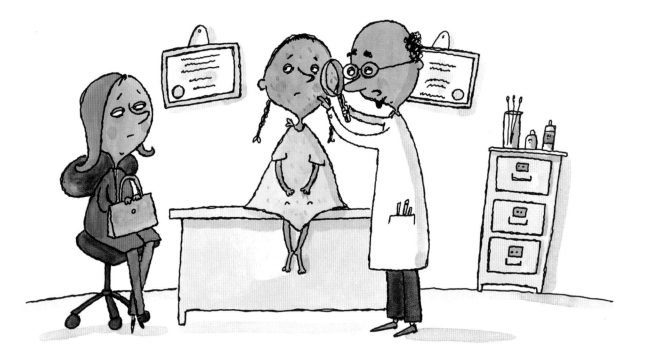

There are many kinds of skin lesions. This word is here so that you can impress your doctor when he asks what's wrong. Instead of pointing to a blister or bump on your skin, you can say with authority, "I have a lesion."

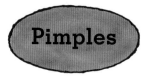

Pimples

A pimple is a raised lump that is filled with pus.
The pus is a sign that infection is causing the trouble.

I have a teenage brother.
Sometimes he has a fit.
He looks into the mirror
And yells, "Egad, a ZIT!"

Cold Sores

A painful red spot that appears around the lips and
sometimes under the nose is usually a cold sore. The
spot gets swollen and oozes, then crusts over. The scab
falls off when the sore beneath it is completely healed.
Cold sores are caused by viruses.

Warts

Warts are little growths on the skin that are also caused by viruses. The virus irritates the underlayers of the skin. The skin reacts by growing a thick, protective covering.

There are many superstitions about what causes warts. The most common is that they come from having a toad pee on you.

I have a little plantar wart
That goes everywhere with me.
It's quite happy on my foot
But I think it's UGH-a-Lee!

A wart is difficult to get rid of. Often the only sure way is to have it removed by a doctor, who may need to treat it more than once.

Here's one of the many superstitions about how to get rid of a wart:

Take the skin of two dead cats.
Go to a graveyard at midnight.
Swing the cat skins over your head three times.
Warts should be gone by morning.

CHAPTER FOUR
Blisters, Bites & Other Skin Troubles NOT Caused by Germs

Blisters

Your skin is made up of three separate layers. A blister is a bubble of watery liquid just under the top layer of skin. The liquid makes the skin above it pop out.

Blisters happen when there is injury to the middle layer of skin, perhaps from rubbing against a tight shoe. The body reacts in its usual way—with inflammation.

Blisters and calluses,
Calluses and blisters,
Leave me alone
And bother my sisters.

Insect Bite

When the stinger of an insect breaks your skin, it causes itching, swelling, and sometimes a lot of pain, especially if it is a bee or wasp bite. Bees and wasps inject poison, and that's why the sting hurts so much.

Mosquitoes buzz.
Mosquitoes bite.
Mosquitoes drive me
wild at night.
Bees buzz.
Bees bite.
A bee sting gives me
quite a fright.

Callus

A callus is hard skin caused by a lot of wear and tear on a foot or a hand. This is the body's special way of keeping the soles of your feet, or the palms of your hands, from getting worn out.

Eczema

Kids with eczema have rough skin on certain parts of their bodies—behind their knees, in the folds of their arms, sometimes on their necks and faces.

The skin feels terribly itchy, and it's hard not to scratch. Eczema is often caused by food allergies. Milk, eggs, and even wheat are common causes of eczema.

There was a teenager from Natchez
Whose skin had bumpy red patches.
Her mom said, "Don't touch!"
But she didn't mind much.
And so when it itches, she scratches!

Sunburn

Whether you get sunburn depends upon the time of day, the season, and your skin's natural protection.

In summer, especially around midday when the sun's rays are the strongest, you are more likely to burn. If you are dark-skinned, it means you have a lot of melanin in your skin, which protects against sunburn. But if your skin is pale and light, it does not have much melanin. Then it is more likely you will be burned by the hot rays of the sun.

It's a good idea for everyone, light or dark, to protect their skin from the sun with sunscreen lotion or protective clothing. Dermatologists tell us that sunburns and suntans are not healthy for the skin.

The day was nice.
The sun was hot.
Now I look like a lobster
Boiled in a pot.

CHAPTER FIVE
Sneezing, Wheezing & Other Allergic Reactions

Sometimes the body gets mixed up and reacts to harmless stuff as if it were dangerous. Then the body's fighting back becomes the trouble.

When you have a sickness caused by germs, your body develops special chemicals, called antibodies, to fight against the germs that are making you sick.

When you have an allergy, your body makes special antibodies, too, but not against germs. Instead, your body makes antibodies against some things that are not usually harmful, such as dust, or cat hair, or various foods. These antibodies then cause trouble every time you eat or come near the thing you are allergic to.

People with allergies have a variety of unpleasant symptoms, such as sneezing, watery eyes, headache, runny nose, rash, and hives. Among the more serious reactions are wheezing and difficulty in breathing.

There are many things people are allergic to, but the one thing that almost everyone is allergic to is poison ivy.

Poison Ivy

The three-leaf poison ivy plant has an oily substance on every part of it—the leaves, the flowers, the roots, and the berries. It's the oily stuff that causes the skin reaction.

I picked some poison ivy.
The leaves were green and pretty.
Now I've got an itchy rash.
Mom says, "What a pity!"

Allergies to Animals

Many people are allergic to animal dander, particularly the dander found in cats and dogs. Some people are also allergic to birds, horses, or rabbits. You name it, and there's probably someone out there who is allergic to it.

I want to have some kitties
To pat until they purr.
I have an awful problem—
I'm allergic to their fur.

Asthma

Asthma is an allergic reaction that causes wheezing and trouble with breathing. People with asthma are often allergic to pollens, molds, dust, and certain animal hairs.

Unfortunately, the number of kids with asthma is growing. Fortunately, there are a number of new medications to help people breathe more easily.

Hay Fever

Hay fever is an allergy to certain pollens and molds. It causes sneezing, runny nose, and itchy eyes.

There's watery stuff pouring out my nose. Would somebody please turn off the hose!

CONCLUSION

Everybody has a body:

>with arms to reach and stretch and hug, and
>fingers to tickle and scratch and hold things

>with legs to walk and skip and climb, feet to kick
>soccer balls, toes to wiggle in the sand

>with eyes to see and ears to hear, a tongue to
>taste, and a mouth to chew and taste and talk

Inside everyone's body are lungs to breathe and a
stomach to digest food, a heart to pump blood, and
a brain to think and to keep the rest of the body
running smoothly.

That makes a lot of opportunities for things to
break down. But most of the time our bodies get
well by themselves. Cuts heal; cold get better; and
headaches stop.

Most illnesses have an "expectable course." They behave in a familiar way. If we rest, drink lots of fluids, and stay warm, even a bad cold gets better.

When an illness doesn't follow the "expectable course," we go to a doctor, who may prescribe medicine. If a cold turns into a bad cough with fever, or a cut gets red and swollen, then the body needs outside help.

Fortunately, our bodies work well enough most of the time, and we hardly notice them as they go about the exciting business of being us.

GLOSSARY

When a car is "sick," it is taken to a muffler shop, an auto body shop, or a mechanic at a garage.

When a body is sick, a person is usually treated by a primary care physician. For some problems, people are sent to specialists. Here are the fancy names for common medical specialties:

allergist – deals with asthma and allergies

dermatologist – treats skin disorders

hematologist – treats blood disorders

neurologist – treats the brain and nervous system

ophthalmologist – eye specialist

orthopedist – treats bones and joints

otolaryngologist – treats ears, nose, and throat

pediatrician – treats babies and children

psychiatrist – treats problems of the mind

radiologist – takes x-rays of the body

surgeon – performs operations

Note to Parents and Caregivers

One of the most difficult and frequent decisions a parent must make is when to take a child to the doctor. In cases of serious injury or severe illness, the decision is not so difficult, and a hospital emergency room is the obvious choice. But when a child complains of not feeling well and there are no clear signs of illness, it can be hard to know what to do. Also, children sometimes complain of feeling sick when they are trying to get out of doing something and when they are not certain themselves if they are really sick. We all have the experience of "not feeling well" and then find that the feeling passes when we get going.

Generally, common sense will tell a caretaker what steps to take with a sick child. A call to the doctor, nurse, or physician's assistant often helps. Sometimes the doctor can help without seeing the child. He or she may say, "It's going around." This means that the office has seen many cases similar to what is being described and that the illness will go away by itself.

One general rule to remember is that most illnesses run an expectable course: colds begin to get better in two to three days; gastrointestinal upsets last a few hours to a day or two; fevers go up and down…and so on. However, if a cold does not improve in two to three days and fever develops with a severe cough, this is not the "expectable course." This is reason to consider calling the doctor.

If a child falls and hits his or her head, there is usually no more concern than a bump and tears. But if the child has been "knocked out" for even a moment, or sleepiness or vomiting ensue, there is cause for serious concern.

Again, common sense and reasonable caution will generally lead to the right decision. What makes decision-making harder is that people approach illness with different levels of anxiety. Part of the art of being a parent is to work out how to deal with emergencies before, not after, they happen. A list of phone numbers and instructions posted on the refrigerator is always a good idea.

Frequently, there is no "correct" decision. A parent has to tolerate the tension between "running to the doctor too often" and managing a problem without seeing a doctor in person. Remaining alert to the changes and the course of an illness and not being hesitant to call the doctor are important. It is also reassuring to know that children have a variety of illnesses and complaints and that the vast majority get better by themselves.

—Dr. Fred Ehrlich